Self-Esteem Your Superpower

Ways Parents Can Improve Children's Self-Esteem

3-2-1 Blast Off

Dr. Stephanie Wilson-Coleman, Ph.D

Library of Congress Registration Number on File
ISBN: 978-0-9749387-9-0 - Paperback

Printed in the United States

Table of Contents

DEDICATION

This book is dedicated to Messiah Mason Henry.

Your love of the solar system is intoxicating.

I know you will reach well beyond the stars.

You Can Do It.

Here's to going to the Moon, Mars, and Jupiter.

I love you more than you will ever know.

And to my Son, Karl Henry.

When we were together in our human bodies, it was always you and me against the world.

Now that you are no longer on this earth plane, the memories will have to carry me through.

Always in my heart.

Always intertwined with my soul.

A child must know that he is a miracle, that since the beginning of the world there hasn't been, and until the end of the world there will not be, another child like him."

Pablo Casals

Introduction

With gladness and joy, I welcome you into the wonderful world of self-esteem. We live in an age where our day-to-day activities contribute to our self-esteem. We have listened to stories about young adults who have lost their lives or done something drastic because of their low level of self-esteem. These stories create fear in us as we think of our children. We do not want to lose them to low self-esteem. So, what do we do to help them develop positive self-esteem? This and many more questions run through our minds as we search for answers.

With this book, we hope this help answer some of your questions you may have concerning self-esteem. We also help you to explore your hidden Superpowers. This book is written by a parent, grandparent, sister, aunt, and cousin for any parent, uncle, aunt, grandparents, siblings, sitters/nannies, or anyone interested in understanding the concept of self-esteem in children. It explains self-esteem, some of the causes of low self-esteem in children, and various techniques to develop positive self-esteem in children, among others.

Join me as we explore the fascinating concept of self-esteem on the pages of this book.

It is time for us to activate our Superpower.

Superheroes Training is in Session

What is Self-Esteem?

Self-esteem can be defined as the overall sense of value, worth, and confidence a person has in himself. It is a feeling that is based on the level of confidence a person has in his worth or abilities. Self-esteem is also based on a person's total perception of himself. It affects one's decision-making and self-assessment process. Self-esteem also includes the feelings people experience that influences their choices and decisions.

Self-esteem can be said to serve as a motivational function, as it heavily influences people's choices and decisions. This is because it is an aspect of people's lives that ensures —if high— that they take care of themselves and explore their full potential. It is important to note that people with high self-esteem do everything to ensure their happiness while striving persistently to fulfill their personal goals and aspirations. High Self-Esteem also helps the community and family by thinking of others with compassion and empathy. On the other hand, people with lower self-esteem tend to be very critical of themselves. They feel they are inferior to their peers and are afraid of making mistakes. They may be less motivated and easily influenced by others' opinions of them.

Self-esteem, also known as self-worth or self-confidence, lies solely in your opinion about yourself. Nothing can determine your level of self-esteem except you. You are the sole influencer of your self-esteem, and your decision can either make or destroy it. It is your overall sense of your abilities and limitations. This is based on what you think you are "worth." It is a subjective assessment of oneself that can be greatly influenced by people's opinions. It determines the worth or value people find in themselves.

A Brief Definition of the Two Types of Self-Esteem

We have heard plenty of people elaborate on the two types of self-esteem and their effects on children. Often, we do not know the differences. As parents, not knowing how to differentiate between these two types of self-esteem can make it difficult to figure out what type of self-esteem our children have. As parents, understanding these concepts helps us better understand our children so we can offer the help needed.

The types of self-esteem are:

High Self-Esteem

High self-esteem is a complete state or frame of mind that allows you to be aware of your strengths and weaknesses and celebrate them. It is a positive mindset that allows you to embrace the hustle and bustle of the day without breaking down or allowing negative activities to defeat you. High self-esteem is related to being open to criticism, acknowledging mistakes, self-love, and confidence in yourself and others.

It is important for parents to note that children with high self-esteem believe greatly that their happiness is from within, and it can only be altered if they allow it. This happens when a child sees real value in him/herself and accepts his/her person. Having higher self-esteem builds a lot of confidence in children, and gives them enough courage to find solutions to problems that come their way. Children with high self-esteem have a great sense of assurance in themselves, which helps them to confidently take risks, or tackle challenges that eventually yield positive results.

One essential thing about children with high self-esteem is the fact that they own up to their actions. These children take responsibility for their own decisions. They do not need constant approval from people to feel good about themselves. Children with high self-esteem are usually open to change and new ideas. This is a result of good communication, networking skills, and the confidence to try new things.

Low Self-Esteem

Low self-esteem is a state of mind where someone lacks confidence about who they are and what they can accomplish. It is characterized by a lack of confidence in one's strengths and abilities. It is the constant feeling of being unlovable and incompetent. Low self-esteem often leads to a fragile sense of self that is caused by being consistently fearful of letting others down and making mistakes.

Children suffering from low self-esteem are easily hurt and offended by the opinions of other people. They often allow the negative opinion of others to influence their thinking process. The most important voice to us is our voice. Children with low self-esteem have a habit of saying negative and critical things about themselves. The brain naturally accepts what we repeatedly say about ourselves. Children who experience low self-esteem think everything that goes wrong is their fault, and they do not have the capabilities to make things right. They doubt their abilities, and this often results in them shying away from or avoiding challenges. Children with low self-esteem think that they do not deserve to be happy, and they feel so unworthy when happy things happen, that they begin to question it.

These issues can result in depression and anxiety. Low self-esteem often harms one's mental health and thinking process.

Causes of Low Self-Esteem in Children

"It is easier to build strong children than to repair broken adults."
— Frederick Douglass

One important thing to note is that a child with low self-esteem grows up to become an adult with poor self-esteem. As adults, they often end up believing they are never good enough and do not deserve to be successful. Parents should strive to understand the causes of low self-esteem. This will help them to understand the various ways by which they can help build self-esteem in their children and possibly in other children. It's said that an ounce of prevention, is worth a pound of cure. You cannot prevent a thing from happening without knowing its cause.

Join me as we explore the various causes of low self-esteem in children and ways to tap into our superpower to help the children in our lives live the best version of themselves.

Bullying

Studies have shown how bullying drastically influences the self-esteem of a child. Bullying affects a child so much that they shy from standing up for themselves and lose their confidence. This can result in a bullied child living in constant fear of the predator. This can increase the tendency to slip into anxiety, sadness, loneliness, loss of confidence, and even mental illness and suicide.

Your Superpower – Communication

Having a close relationship with your children is key. Communication matters. Listen to your child and give them your full attention – no phone, no television, no electronic devices. Just you and your child. Use this time just to talk. Below are a few conversation starters:

- Talk about their day.
- What made them laugh, sad, or angry?
- What interesting fact did they learn?
- What is your favorite thing to do in the car?
- If we were in the grocery store, what would you buy?

- If you could make three wishes, what would they be?
- What's your favorite smell? Your least liked smell?
- If you could be a pizza which one, would you be?
- Tell me about...?
- How would you change...?
- What would happen if we...?
- How does it work?

These are just some suggestions. Many more can be found on the internet. Do not be afraid to use your imagination to create your own questions.

Your Superpower – Play

Playtime allows you and your child to activate your imagination, and creativity creates a strong emotional bond and promotes physical fitness.

Participation in activities such as Hide and Seek, Scavenger Hunts, Sidewalk Chalk Art, and walks in the park. Play word games, and board games, make up jokes, paint, and color together. The list is endless and filled with fun.

Children are different so do your best to find activities your child will enjoy. This allows you and your children to bond and have fun.

Have fun experimenting.

Your Superpower – Empathy

When your children make derogatory comments about themselves, make sure you are understanding and compassionate. Negate their negative self-talk by acknowledging their feelings, not the words, use role-playing for the funniest situation, and encourage them to think of new ways to solve their problem. Ask interesting and open-ended questions to discover how they're doing in school, church, or even play groups. Instead of asking how your day was, ask:

- What was your favorite activity in school today?
- Who inspires you the most and why?
- In what way can you...?
- I wonder what will happen if we...? How does it work?
- Tell me about a time when you felt left out?
- Look at your child and ask, "What are you thinking right now"?
- Encourage your child to keep a journal.

Your Superpower – Confidence

One easy way to help children exude confidence is to teach them how to use their body language to exude confidence. Teach them the "Superman Pose."

Using powerful body language, such as standing tall and placing their hands on their waist and using words such as "stop, I don't like that." Teach them not to allow any form of disrespect from anyone.

These are just a few techniques.

Comparison ... Nah...instead Try Celebrating their Progress

Your Superpower – Celebration

Numerous parents see the comparison to others as an opportunity to entice their children to work harder —especially in academics.

Constantly comparing your child to other children is another way to damage self-esteem.

The unhealthy comparison tends to lower one's self-worth. Judging a child for being different from other children makes him feel less of himself and can also diminish their passion. It does not matter if others are better. What matters is their effort, what they learned, and what they enjoyed. The key is to help children identify their own hard work and successes. Celebrate their process and their achievements.

Here are a few tips to help you celebrate your child's success:

- Create a victory tradition
- Share the success with family, friends, and colleagues
- Spend quality time with your child

Remember, you can create your own.

Go, Team Go! V-I-C-T-O-R-Y! Go Team Go

Emotionally Distant Parents – Tips to Reconnect

Childhood brings its own set of successes, failures, laughter, sorrow, good times, and not-so-good times. Childhood is the perfect storm for a rollercoaster ride filled with emotional issues. Being dismissive about the child's emotional life aids in further reducing that child's self-esteem.

Unfortunately, bullying, including cyberbullying, continues to rise. With the increase in bullying, the constant use of electronic devices may result in a child becoming emotionally distant from their parents.

Parents, our Superheroes, must remain diligently on "watch" duty. Watch duty can include establishing a time to spend together as a family game night; unplugging electronics at a set time; one-on-one time engaging in arts & crafts; walks in the park; visits to animal shelters. You will be amazed by the number of free activities available for you and your children.

Your Superpower: Knowing When You Need to Turn for Help.

Abuse – Time to Signal for Help

Abuse has a debilitating effect on humans, and if the emotional scars go untreated, it can affect the person in all areas of their life. Self-esteem is not excluded. An abused child can have very low self-esteem, because of the trauma they have experienced. A child who experiences a constant pattern of physical abuse by parents will see abuse as a normal thing and often protect their parents, fearing further abuse if authorities are notified. This can result in the child becoming prey to bullies. The emotions of negativity bias are more powerful than positivity bias. Because of this, Psychologists have proven that trauma has long lingering effects. Physical abuse will prevent the child from speaking up for himself. Like physical abuse, emotional and sexual abuse have drastic effects, especially on children. Sexually abused children carry the trauma from the abuse for a long time and may develop PTSD. This increases their feeling of being unloved and unwanted. They grow up feeling the world is unsafe, they are not worthy, and no one can be trusted.

As a Superhero, if you suspect a child is being abused, contact the Childhelp National Abuse Hotline (800) 422-4453 or https://childhelphotline.org/ for guidance. You can also contact Clergy and/or Professional Counselors for help.

Academic Difficulties

A child who has difficulties in any academic area may be prone to a drop in self-esteem. Competence is one attribute that can increase self-esteem in some children. Feeling they are not "smart" enough to succeed in school also reduces the feeling of being competent, which plays a great role in reducing the child's self-esteem. This could cause the child to become reluctant to do their best and hinder their academic growth.

When children are experiencing academic difficulties, you can help them by:

- Help them identify their strengths and weakness.
- Celebrate that all people are different.
- Always praise effort and not the outcome.
- Learn how your child learns - visual, auditory kinesthetic. Experiment with each type.
- Set goals.
- Work with various professionals to diagnose the difficulty, so you know how to respond.
- Do your own research. Take charge of finding tools and tactics to best help your child learn.

Family Conflict

Family conflict can be another cause of low self-esteem in children. Growing up in a situation or a family that is filled with violence, or any form of abuse has a great effect on the mental health of children. Parental conflicts can cause some children to withdraw. When a family is going through a permanent change, finding ways to discuss these changes with the children will help minimize any negative effects.

The "family" plays a key role in a child's life. The family unit is the first unit to shape the child's self-esteem. The more the child feels love, the better their self-esteem. Families with constant turmoil greatly benefit from various counseling techniques.

Of course, different children require different techniques. Feel free to experiment to determine which will work best for your child.

A few techniques you can try are

- Positive physical contact – hugs & kisses. Remember, research shows that when you hug, hold the hug for 20 seconds and more. This allows time to boost the immune system and reduce stress.
- Praise and actively listen to your child.
- Set high and achievable expectations.

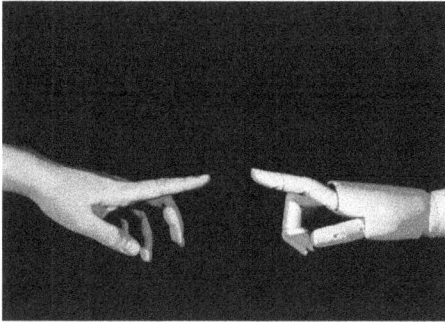

"The Future is worth it.
All the Pain. All the Tears
The Future is Worth the fight."

Martian Manhunter

Let's Do This!
SUPERHEROES
ASSEMBLE –
With great power comes
great responsibility.

Siblings with Very Different Experiences –
The Story of Daniel and Melody

Daniel has always struggled in school. He had difficulty with math and science but excelled in sports. He's on the varsity basketball team, which requires he maintain a minimum of a C average in all his classes. His success in basketball and teamwork with teachers, coaches, and parents help keep him motivated in class.

Daniel has a great personality. Everyone loves him. He is kind, respectful, and has a great sense of humor. He is always willing to help others. However, academics were a significant challenge for him. Daniel's mom was clear regarding her expectations. Daniel had to maintain good grades in order to participate in extracurricular activities, such as sports.

Daniel is aware that he can ask for help anytime he needs it. He also knows that his mom will not relax her requirements – participating in sports requires him to make good grades. No excuses were allowed. The consequences for failure are clear – no basketball.

Daniel's coach is invested in both his academic and sports success. He encourages Daniel to do his best both on the court and off. When he fails or makes mistakes, his Coach and Mom help him process the experience and learn what he can from it.

Daniel is so motivated by playing basketball that he gives 100% in the classroom.

However, at times, he makes failing grades in math.

When Daniel's favorite aunt died, he had difficulty sleeping, and focusing in class. He kept up his homework but started failing math tests. The week before homecoming, Daniel received an F on his report card. The loss of his favorite aunt was very difficult for Daniel.

Daniel accepted responsibility for making a failing grade and understood he would need to sit out until mid-term grades were reported.

Daniel was able to dress out for games; however, he would have to sit on the bench. Daniel never missed practice and continued to support the team. He also asked to do extra credit work in math, which helped bring his grade point average up.

Daniel's mom realized that basketball was his motivation for keeping up his grades and largely how he managed to feel confident despite academic challenges.

She also knew that not following through with these consequences would be failing Daniel. The delicate balance between succeeding in sports and accountability in schoolwork contributed to his positive self-esteem. It took a whole team of adults with Daniel's best interest at heart to make this work.

Melody, Daniel's sister, was an entirely different story. She was the youngest child and only girl. From a young age, she received extra attention from everyone in her household. Academics and school were easy for Melody, and she excelled in every class.

Melody delved into academics but was not interested in any other activities. She did love animals and hurried home from school to play with their animals. They had two dogs, Blaze and Milo. The pets were kept in another part of the house while Melody completed her homework.

Melody's parents were not in agreement on parenting. Mom was responsible for ensuring Daniel completed his homework and household chores, however, Dad would often allow Melody to play with the pets and skip study time and household chores.

The consequences of not caring for Blaze and Milo were clear – Melody would clean up any messes. When Melody neglected to take the dog out for walks and potty breaks as agreed, Dad cleaned up the mess when Mom was not around.

Despite her academic gifts, Melody did not have a strong interest in school. She could not identify how she was special or different from the other high achievers attending her school. The thought of continuing higher education was of no interest to her. She was most interested in pursuing her love of animals. Melody began to be late for school. The school officials were concerned. Her grades begin to slip. Melody's grades also suffered when her aunt died.

After working with the school officials, the family started counseling. The parent understood that they must address their children's self-esteem. The parents agreed they must be in agreement on rules, and consequences and follow through.

They agreed that Daniel would help Melody accept responsibility for her choices by spending more time talking with her when she needed support.

Melody was allowed to start volunteering at the local rescue animal center when her academics and chores were completed. This served as a great motivator for Melody. Her academic performance improved greatly.

Both Daniel and Melody are now performing successfully in school and at home.

Fall from Grace

The Story Behind the Fallen Superstar, Mackenzie

Mackenzie was a lovely 13-year-old girl, full of life and vigor. At 13, Mackenzie was in the 10th grade, having skipped two grades. This teenage girl was the epitome of beauty, intelligence, and any other good attributes you can think of. Since the day she started school at Saint John School, she was loved by teachers, and even non-teaching staff because of her good manners. In addition to her good manners, she was well known for her intelligence. Being the brightest child in her school, the board of teachers agreed that she should be promoted to a higher class as her intelligence was beyond her present class. She was indeed charming and loved by all.

One would expect that Mackenzie would be getting equal attention both at home and at school, but this is not the case. Instead, at home, she is a loner and spent all her time in her room wishing she could receive the same amount of love from her mother that she received from her nanny. Being the only child of her wealthy parents did not help at all. They were rarely around. Her father was always flying out of the country for one business trip or the other. Her mother, on the other hand, spends time attending various high-end events. These two important people in Mackenzie's life were almost always absent from her life. On her last birthday, Mackenzie thought she would spend the day with her mother, whom she expected to tell her all she needed to know about being a teenager, but her mom got an eleventh-hour invitation to an event and left her daughter all to herself. Because of this, Mackenzie resented her parents and became a loner.

One day, a new girl came to her school and captured the attention of almost everyone. In the hallways, in the lunchroom, at the basketball court, in every corner of the school, everyone was talking about this new girl. Suddenly, Mackenzie the star of the school became invisible to everyone. This new girl, Helena, became the talk of the school. Even the principal commended the girl's brilliance in front of the whole school. Mackenzie felt her entire world crumbling at her feet. The thing she found solace in —the attention showered on her by everyone in the school— was transferred to another person in school. That attention was her only source of happiness, and now that it is gone, she hated school more than she hated her home.

Her grades began to drop drastically. She began to lose interest in school —her only haven— and mingled with teenagers that were known troublemakers. She became very aggressive and grew from the sweet little girl everyone once knew to a bully. Her new set of friends were bullies, and the only way to gain their validation was to become a bully like them.

The school authorities noticed the sudden change in their former superstar and called her parents. Her parents, who were never around, found it a bit difficult to honor the school's invitation. They kept postponing their visit to the school anytime they were invited by the school for a talk. Little did they know that their little princess was begging for validation from the wrong people, and these people were influencing her decisions.

One day, Mackenzie's mother came back from one of her numerous events and found her teenage daughter, looking like a shadow of her old self. Mackenzie has lost a lot of weight and was looking thin and hopeless. She was shocked beyond words and quickly called her nanny and the school authorities and accused them both of being the cause of her daughter's downward spiral.

Mackenzie's nanny explained to her mother all that has been happening, how Mackenzie kept withdrawing from others, and how she barely talked to others. The school authorities also explained their part of the story, how her grades have been dropping and reminded Mackenzie's mother of the numerous meetings they tried to schedule with her and Mackenzie's father.

Mackenzie was introduced to therapy. The therapist encouraged Mackenzie to open up and discuss her feelings. The therapist also worked with both parents and Mackenzie's nanny. Using various techniques taught by the therapist, her parents were successful in finding creative ways to become emotionally close to their daughter.

Epilogue
Superhero: Your Call to Action

Let's Do This - We Can Do This All Day Long

Self-Esteem Experiment

The self-esteem experiment or movement started in 1969. This movement began with the use of Nathaniel Braden's "The Psychology of Self-Esteem." This movement aimed to produce an increase in the rate of the citizen's self-esteem, to make them more productive. In this movement, a task force was set up, which included parenting experts and a few people. The idea of the whole movement is to form a group that collectively supports the use of 'praises' as a commendation for good works, and ignoring, and downplaying any form of failure. In this experiment, school authorities changed the grading system in schools. The experiment discourages the idea of failing and passing, which was the normal grading system in schools. Instead, they changed the normal grading system of failing and passing to giving encouraging remarks like "satisfactory," "exceeded expectations," "needs improvement," and so on. The point of the experiment was to stop acknowledging failure. Furthermore, extracurricular activities like sports were changed from being competitive to being cooperative. So, competitors became cooperators.

As time passed, the organizers of this project realized the project failed. They realized that commending people for their intelligence is not enough; instead, intelligence must be coupled with hard work. The project revealed one important truth – intelligence alone will not guarantee success. Success requires hard work, sacrifice, diligence, perseverance, and the ability to accept criticism. Removing accountability and expectations from children did not improve their performance at all. Instead, it indirectly taught the children that hard work was not important.

It is important to focus on recognition and praise, but by removing accountability and expectations, children are taught that hard work is not important. This approach indirectly teaches children that they do not need to put more work into achieving their goals. In other words, it is essential to reward people or children whenever they perform a task impressively, however, it causes problems when they are rewarded for just showing up.

This experiment supported the idea of rewarding children for just showing up without putting in the effort to gain something. This will teach the child that just showing up without any real commitment will guarantee success.

To help a child improve their self-esteem, you must teach them that showing up, and doing their best is key. If not, they must face the consequences of not being prepared. Success occurs when you have self-confidence, and the ability to accept criticism when wrong.

How to Develop High Self-Esteem in Your Children

To develop positive and stable self-esteem in your children, it is essential for you as a parent to understand the concept of self-esteem. Self-esteem is not learned or given as a gift, instead, it is built unconsciously. It is fostered by equipping them with skills that help to build their self-confidence. Teach your child that it is okay and very normal to fail, but what is not okay is not doing your best, and not taking the necessary steps to prepare. As parents, we have to give our children the freedom to make choices. Allow them to make decisions and fail if necessary. Teach them what to do if failure arises. Encourage them to check in with you often to discuss options.

Here are a few steps that can help you develop positive self-esteem in your children.

Communicate Your Expectations

This cannot be overemphasized. Spell out the expectations to your children clearly. Discuss the consequences and rewards for their actions.

- Explain how you want them to be accountable for these expectations
- Make sure both of you agree on the terms of this expectation
- Outline specifically for them what needs to be done and how they should do it
- Check in with them regularly to gauge their success, needs, or difficulty

Get All Adults in the Child's Life Onboard

- Explain the importance of being consistent with your expectations

- Discuss clear rules and regulations, and the consequences the child will face

Your Child's life is filled with adults that function as your support system. This support system includes grandparents, siblings, uncles, aunts, or even sitters/nannies that have a connection with your child. At this point in your journey to developing positive esteem in your child, you need all the support you can get from them.

Follow Through with Your Expectations Consistently, and Discuss Any Changes

Your children will need to take responsibility for their actions and deeds. You are also responsible for yours. If you stated in your expectations that you would do something to ensure they meet the expectations, do it. Be consistent with your side of the deal. Being inconsistent sends a signal that tells your children that the issue is not important and that you cannot be trusted to follow your commitments.

The result of being inconsistent is indirectly giving your children an opportunity to ignore their part of the agreement and to slack off.

Allow Them to Accept Challenges, and, if Possible, Face the Natural Consequences of Failing

Some parents have a tendency to be too overprotective. They are overprotective to the extent that they try to protect their children from taking up challenges, that may end up as failures. Parents are human beings also, so try to remember that as parents, you only have so much control over another human. Always controlling your children, or shielding them from challenges, can be detrimental to the self-esteem of the child. You must be willing to allow them to accept challenges and experience failure.

Furthermore, you must be willing to let them face the natural consequences of some actions —failing. Allow them to take up challenges in their way.

As parents, we only want our children to experience good things, successes, and happy times. You must help them understand that you win some and you lose some. There is only one 1st place winner.

The Beauty of Failure. Turn Mistakes Into Teachable Moments.

Failure teaches us what we do not know about ourselves. It teaches us how we learn and how we grow. It teaches us what does not work, and what does work.

It creates valuable opportunities for us to learn. It does the same for all ages, for all people.

Allowing your child to handle responsibilities their own way and fail is important. Let your child know that failing is inevitable, but remaining a failure is a choice.

Have conversations that discuss what you would have done differently in that situation. Discuss ways they can handle the situation to avoid failing the next time.

You help them by talking about their mistakes, what they learned, and what they could do better next time.

That is why communicating with your children is crucial to gaining positive self-esteem. Let them discuss the choices they made and the lessons they learned from their failure.

Lovingly explain that you are talking about the choices they made. You are not disappointed in them.

Perhaps asking the question, "what has become clear to you?" will help them think about the action they took and the action they need to take in the future.

Reward Good Behaviors and Reprimand Bad Behaviors

Accolades and praises have an incredibly brilliant effect on the minds of people – especially children. It provides a turbo-boost to their self-esteem. Compliment and praise your children whenever they meet their goals, and your expectations, and perform well. Tell them you appreciate their efforts and watch how your words will enhance your children's day. Be generous with words whenever you feel pleased with their behavior.

In the same vein, do not hesitate to correct or reprimand whenever your child does something wrong or fails to meet your expectations. Correct with love while holding your stance as a parent. Try using the sandwich approach – praise, criticize, praise.

Steps to Build a Praise Sandwich

Praise your child

- Compliment (positive):
    - o Specifically compliment your child on recent behavior.

Criticize

- Address the issues or negative behavior

Praise

- Compliment (positive)
    - o End the conversation with a compliment for a different good behavior

Be Their Trusted Partner and Trusted Parent

Below are a few techniques to help you be present in your child's life.

- Watch their favorite shows together
- Play their favorite game together
- Take them to their favorite places
- Take time to "cook" with them
- Find ways they can help you with your work
- Schedule arts and crafts together (remember everyone can color)

Take the time to know what is going on with your child in school, or anywhere you might not be. Protect your child from bullying and any form of vices that can make your child's self-esteem decline. Be emotionally available to your children, constantly ask them how they feel about school, who's the new child at school, and what made you laugh today? These questions help to start a conversation. With these conversations, you will get to know what is going on with your child.

Let love be the reigning theme between you and your child and watch your child's self-esteem grow.

"You're going to make a difference. A lot of times it won't be huge, it won't be visible even. But it will matter just the same."

James Gordon

ABOUT THE AUTHOR

Featured on WGN-TV Daytime Chicago, UpJourney Magazine, Authority Magazine, The Crusader, N'digo Magazine, MetaMonthly Magazine, Dr. Stephanie E. Wilson-Coleman is a highly sought-after speaker, Holistic Life Coach turned Executive Leadership Coach, author of 4 books, host of the popular podcast, A Sip of Inspiration, and Founder and CEO of The Champagne Connection. (www.champagneconnection.com). Dr. Stephanie has an Executive M.B.A from the University of Chicago Booth, Ph.D. in Holistic Life Counseling, and a Behavioral Finance Certification from Duke University.

Dr. Stephanie is a teenage mother, a survivor of sexual molestation, gang rape, homelessness, and experience a near-death experience when diagnosed with a basal skull fracture. She has the uncanny ability to help others transform obstacles into stepping stones to living their dreams.

Let Dr. Stephanie help you find the winning strategy in the cards life has dealt. For more information visit: www.champagneconnection.com

www.ingramcontent.com/pod-product-compliance
Lightning Source LLC
Chambersburg PA
CBHW042338040426
42447CB00017B/3471